The Publisher would like to thank the following for their contribution
in the compiling of this book:

John Hammond of Crawley R.F.C.
Peter Smith
Members of LUAS and the SLOBS

'The Early Days of Rugby Football' was taken from 'How The
Game Began'. This book is available from the author. For details
please contact the publisher and we will forward your enquiry.

Special thanks to Ron Fry of Shirley Wanderers R.F.C. without whose
enthusiasm and encouragement this book would not
have been possible.

Printed in England by Panda Press

Folio © 1991 International Music Publications
Southend Road · Woodford Green · Essex IG8 8HN · England
215-2-625

RUGGER OFF

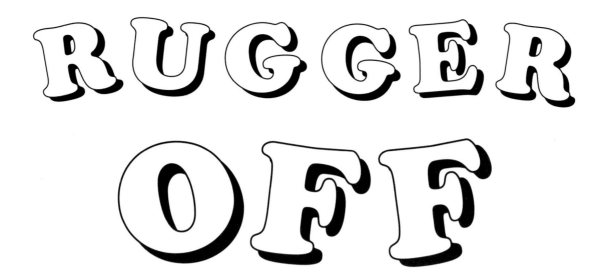

The Early Days of Rugby Football

The Origins

The origins are shrouded in mystery and legend. In very early days, it is believed that some form of game took place, in which an object of undetermined shape was contested between a "great number of persons, divided into two parties, opposed to each other." A game called 'Harpastum,' a word derived from the Greek word meaning to "seize," is known to have been played by the Romans. "Seize" obviously implies that some carrying of the ball was allowed. The game, it is believed, was played indoors. A large group of players was divided; an area was marked with lines at each end and a dividing line in the middle; a ball was thrown up between the two sets of players, who tried to carry it beyond their opponents line. One can conclude that the scrummaging that inevitably took place, was the origin of the scrum and that there was handling of the ball. Another game played in Italy and out of doors, using an inflated follis or bladder, has been played in Tuscany from the Middle Ages to modern times.

Early Games in Britain

During the Middle Ages, in England, there are records of young men leaving their work at certain times, such as Shrove Tuesday, to compete with each other over some sort of ball. In Tudor days laws were made against football, described as a "devilish pastime" which resulted in "murther homicide and great effusion of blood, as experience daily teacheth."

Shrove Tuesday became in many parts of the country, an occasion for such games of mass football. In some games, kicking was allowed; in others, it was strictly forbidden. Glover in his "History of Derbyshire", written in 1829 writes of a game in Derby which gave rise to the expression 'local Derby'. "The players are young men from 18-30 or upwards; married as well as single and many veterans who retain a relish for the sport are occasionally seen in the very heat of the conflict . . About noon a large ball is tossed up in the middle of them . . . This is seized upon by some of the strongest and most active men of each party. The rest of the players close in upon them and a solid mass is formed. It then becomes the object of each party to impel the course of the crowd towards their particular goal.

An early medieval street game.

"At Corfe Castle, Dorset, a pig's bladder was kicked for 31 1/2 miles - to establish a right of way for the marble cutters to transport their stone to barges. More competitive games, involving considerable physical injuries took place, leaving a trail of "broken heads, broken shins, torn coats and hats," as opponents strove to drive the ball towards a goal.

Often the "pitch" was rough and long - the ball being driven or carried over fields, hedges, ditches, streams or through town streets. Strategies, such as hiding the ball, ambushing the parties in possession, were employed. No doubt in some areas, there were basic attempts to codify a regional game - for instance, kicking the ball was banned in some areas of Scotland. There is even a record in some areas that it was forbidden to "deal forballe" - to pass a ball forward, a significant step towards the modern game of rugby.

The Early Game at Rugby

Rugby School was founded in 1574 by the benefaction of Lawrence Sheriff, a local townsman, who prospered in London, as grocer to Queen Elizabeth I. He left money and property "for a fair and convenient school house and for maintaining an honest and discreet and learned man, chosen and appointed to teach grammar freely in the same school." The site was in the centre of the town of Rugby, opposite the church of St. Andrew's, until 1749, when the school moved to the present position because the original buildings were proving inadequate; there was no playground for the boys. The only piece of ground available, was just beyond the churchyard, very small, and certainly not a suitable place for indulging in the rough type of football game that was being played in so many parts of England by then. The new school, however, was well endowed with playing space and in the early 19th Century, a game, similar in some ways to the Shrove Tuesday spectacle, that included rough handling of the opponents and hacking at legs, but very little handling of the ball, was being played on the Close. Originally games took place on the North West side, where the chapels are today, but the building of the first Chapel necessitated a move to the field south of the Headmaster's garden wall, which was known as Old Bigside.

An Early Game on the Close

Matthew Holbeche Bloxham, the famous Rugby antiquarian, gives us a description of the game as played in 1817. "When all assembled in the Close, two of the best players in the school commenced choosing, one for each side. After choosing about a score for each side, a some- what rude division was made of the remaining fags, half of whom were sent to keep goal on one side, the other half to the opposite goal for the same purpose. Any fag, though not chosen, might follow up on that side to the goal of which he was attached."

The number of boys playing in a game on Big Side could be almost as many as two hundred. The early lithograph that follows, shows sides picked numbering about forty each."Some of these were ready enough to mingle in the fray; others judiciously kept half back, watching their opportunity for a casual kick, which was not infrequently afforded them. Few and simple were the rules of the game; touch on the sides of the ground was marked out and *no one was allowed to run with the ball* in his grasp towards the opposite goal. It was football and not handball, plenty of hacking but little struggling.

As to costume, there were neither flannels nor caps. The players simply dropped their hats, coats and jackets, which were heaped together on either side near the goals until the game was over. All were scratch matches, one boarding house was never pitted against each other . . . After the games of the day were concluded (Author's note - Evidence is available that games were continued over several days. All matches were considered drawn after five days - or after three days, if no goal had been kicked!) however vigorously they were contested, all further semblance of the game was consigned to the limbo of oblivion; our tasks at night were sufficiently onerous to allow us little leisure for discussion".

The Webb Ellis Story

It was Matthew Bloxham, who also provides an account of the famous occasion in 1823 when "with a fine disregard for the rules of the game as played in his time, William Webb Ellis first took the ball in his arms and ran with it, thus originating the distinctive feature of the Rugby game."

Bloxham writes "In the latter half of 1823, some fifty-seven years ago, originated, though without pre-meditation, that change in one of the rules, which more than any other has since distinguished the Rugby School game from the Association rules. A boy of the name of Ellis—William Webb Ellis - a town boy and a foundationer, who at the age of nine entered the school after the mid-summer holidays in 1816, who in the second year of 1823 was, I believe a praeposter (a monitor at the school), while playing Big side at football in that half-year, caught the ball in his arms. This being so, according to the then rules, he ought to have retired back; as far as he pleased, without parting with the ball, for the combatants on the opposite side could only advance to the spot where he had caught the ball and were unable to rush forward until he had punted it or placed it for someone to kick, for it was by means of these place kicks at goal that most of the goals were kicked. But, the moment it touched the ground, the opposite side might rush on. Ellis, for the first time disregarded this rule and on catching the ball, instead of retiring backward, rushed forward with the ball in his hands towards the opposite goal, with what result as to the game I know not, neither do I know how this infringement of a well known rule was followed up, or when it became, as it is now, the standing rule."

Matthew Bloxham goes on to describe William Webb Ellis as a boy who was high up in the school and of fair average abilities. He was not "a swell", but there was no lack of assurance with him and he was ambitious of being thought well of."

His life history is summarised as follows:-

1807 - Born in Manchester to James Ellis and his wife Ann (Née Webb.) The second son.

1809 - His father bought a commission in the 3rd Dragoon Guards.

1812 - Father killed in action at Battle of Albuera. His mother moved to Rugby, so that her sons could attend Rugby School.

1816 - Webb Ellis entered Rugby School.

1823 - As a praeposter, he played in the match and showed his "fine disregard for the rules."

1825 - Entered Brasenose College, Oxford as an exhibitioner.

Later took holy orders, became minister of St. George's church Albermarle St. in London and then of the famous St Clement's Dane church. For the last 17 years of his life was Rector of Lower Magdalen Church in Essex.

1872 - Died in Menton in France.

Until 1959 William Webb Ellis's death has been a mystery. In that year his grave was tracked down by Mr Ross McWhirter, in the cemetery of the Vieux Chateau at Menton. Pleased that he was buried on French soil, the French Rugby Union renovated the grave and it is now cared for by local enthusiasts.

The 1895 Enquiry into the Origins of the Game

The contribution of William Webb Ellis to the modern game was carefully examined by the 1895 sub-committee of Old Rugbeians "to, enquire into the Origin of Rugby Football." This committee examined contributions from Old Rugbeians who were either contemporaries or near contemporaries of the innovator. The game before Webb Ellis was "not the game that Rugby

knows now, but something more resembling Association" the report said. A Mr Harris who left the school in 1828 wrote that "picking up and running with the ball in hand was forbidden.

"If the player caught the ball on a rebound from the ground, he could attempt a drop kick at goal, subject to interference from opponents. If he caught the ball from a kick - a fair catch - he was entitled to a "place try" at goal, from any point behind where the catch was made and without interference .

Mr Harris claimed that when someone ran with the ball, it was regarded as unfair by the others and the perpetrator was very liable to be 'hacked over'. Another contributor to the enquiry—A Rev Francis Hugh Dean (1830-1839) relates that certain celebrated kickers and fast runners waited outside scrummages, ready to make a 'drop' for goal. Running with the ball was tolerated if the ball was taken "on the bound." The famous Thomas Hughes, author of "Tom Brown's School Days" made the contribution that "a jury of Rugby boys of that day would almost certainly have found a verdict of justifiable homicide if a boy had been killed in "running in." He went on to add that the question of "running in" was finally settled in 1841/2, when it became legalised provided (a) the ball was caught on the bound (b) the catcher was not "off his side" (c) that the catcher did not pass the ball but ran on in himself.

It is now generally accepted that the innovative nature of William Webb Ellis was to provide the distinctive feature to a game that is beloved, played and watched by men and women of all classes and of every trade and profession.

Hacking

One of the least attractive elements of the game at Rugby School was "hacking." This was, without a doubt a very brutal part of the game. It consisted simply of 'hacking' the other man off his legs by sheer brute force and with certain mechanical aids. A player in 1839 writes, "The custom of the big boys was, at the beginning of the football season, to send a pair of boots to the shoemakers in order to have thick soles put to them, bevelled at the toes (like a man of war's bows) so as to cut into the shins of the enemy. Often I have seen boys thus lamed, sitting on the seats under the elm trees, disabled from further playing."

The scientific "hack over" was not a hard kick. It was a gentle glancing kick, which, if it caught the oncoming opponent at the right place (about three inches above the ankle), on the front of the shin - brought him down "like a shot rabbit" violently on to his face. The following description of hacking is in "The Three Friends", a novel written by an old Rugbeian, which never achieved the popularity of "Tom Brown's Schooldays", but gives some idea of the brutality of hacking.

The fifth formers set out to settle a score against Potter, a renowned scrummager, playing for the Sixth against the rest of the School. When they found him "he did not flinch. Once he came upon their outside number and feeling his assault, returned it with a kick like that of a mad bullock, and passed on unheeding . . . At last when in the thickness of the press, he met them full in front, then ensued a conflict which we will not describe particularly. Enough to say that all thought of the game as a game was forgotten and the private vendetta was fought out to the bitter end. Even after the scrummage was over, the fight still continued and the avengers carried away marks which, however honourable as scars, were none the less painful and disabling. Some of the scars of football, it is said, men carry to their graves." This brutal aspect of the game, which would undoubtedly have inhibited its popular growth, was abolished in 1871, the year of the formation of the Rugby Union.

A drawing of an early form of scrummaging on the Close.

From the School to the World

Steeped in the traditions and customs of their school, it was only natural that Rugbeians should spread the gospel of the game. Many old boys went to Oxbridge universities and gradually the game became more established in both places.

The first university match was in 1872 and not surprisingly on the field from two sides of twenty each - the Oxford XX and Cambridge XX -twenty-four of the players were Old Rugbeians.

From the universities, Old Rugbeians went into the schools as teachers and introduced their game to such places as Marlborough, Clifton and Wellington. These venues meant that at first the game was the prerogative of the 'privileged' classes, but, at first in the North of England, and later in the South, the competitive nature of the game appealed to working class men and fixture lists were soon compiled.

The game was soon to spread to all the Home countries. In Scotland there is a record of a game in 1851, but it was not until 1873, that the Scottish Rugby Union was founded. In Ireland there was competition from both Gaelic and Association football, but by 1879 the Irish Football Union had been formed, whilst in 1878, the South Wales Football Club became the South Wales Football Union. Overseas development can perhaps be mostly attributed to the activities of the Services, who played the game all over the world and inspired indigenous populations with their enthusiasm. In Australia. as early as 1864, a university team in Sydney played against a Royal navy team from visiting British warships. An Australian Rugby Football Union was formed as late as 1949. New Zealand participation in the game first started in 1870 when an ex-pupil of Sherbourne School converted, by sheer enthusiasm, clubs playing Association rules, to the Rugby game. South Africa and France were soon to follow. By 1989 - the year of the preliminaries of the 1991 Rugby World Cup, besides those aforementioned - Czechoslovakia, Rumania, Yugoslavia, Portugal, W. Germany, the Netherlands, Spain, Belgium, Poland, the Ivory Coast, Morocco, Tunisia, Zimbabwe, Malaysia, Hong Kong, Taiwan, Sri Lanka, Korea, Japan, Tonga, Russia, Western Samoa, the U.S.A., Canada, Sweden, Argentina, and many other countries, are playing Rugby football.

The Ball

The history of the ball used in the game is enshrined in the fascinating James Gilbert Rugby Football Museum in St. Matthew Street, Rugby. The museum is a treasure trove of fascinating photographs, documents and artefacts, all relating to the game of Rugby Football and its association with the Rugby School. Displays contain memorabilia, from many British rugby clubs and rugby playing countries including international caps and shirts etc. William Gilbert, maker of the boots and shoes to Rugby School, moved into the premises in 1842 and was succeeded by his nephew James. James is described as a "delightful man", much loved by the boys of the school of his time. He used to blow up the footballs by mouth and an old Rugbeian refers to his powerful lungs and how he used to scour the countryside for the pigs' bladders which, surrounded by four pieces of cowhide, were the balls used by the School. He was, incidentally also famous for his 'tweakers', or catapults, which he made for the schoolboys, until they were outlawed. It was the rather elongated shape of the pig's bladder that led to the oval shape of the rugby ball. In Tom Brown's Schooldays we read in the description of a Bigside Game, "the new ball you may see lie there, quite by itself, in the middle, pointing towards the School or island goal". This an obvious reference to the elongated shape of the ball. It was another Rugby townsman, Richard Lindon, a boot, shoe and football maker from Lawrence Sheriff Street, who is considered to be the inventor of the 'India Rubber Football Bladder' and also the brass pump for inflating them. Alas, for him, he did not patent his inventions and other manufacturers made similar bladders and pumps at about the same time. The early ball was very suitable for long drop kicking, for place kicking and for dribbling, but as the game developed into more of a handling and passing game, the shape of the ball was changed, to make it more suitable for these aspects. The Rugby Football Museum has a fascinating show case, which shows the development of the ball from a pig's bladder to the Gilbert "Barbarian ball", which includes all the latest Gilbert technology. The firm has developed a wet friction coating for the leather laminate ball, which handles superbly in all weather. It was not until 1892 that the size and shape of the ball were written into the rules, but some variations are possible and it is interesting to note that in New Zealand the ball usually measures half an inch less in width than in the United Kingdom.

The First Attempt to Codify the Game

Resolutions

That only in cases of extreme emergency, and only by the permission of the heads of the sides, shall any one be permitted to leave the Close, after calling over, till the game be finished, and consequently, that all dressing take place before that time.

That the punishment for absenting oneself from a match, without any real and well-ground reason, be left to the discretion of any Praeposter.

That whenever a match is going to be played, the School shall be informed of it by the Head of the School in such manner as he shall think fit, some time before dinner on the day in question.

That no unnecessary delay take place in the commencement of the matches, but as soon as calling over be finished the game be commenced.

That the old custom, that no more than two matches take place in the same week be strictly adhered to, of which one must always take place on Saturday, without some strong cause to the contrary.

That all fellows not following up, strictly prohibited from playing any game in goal, or otherwise conducting themselves in any way which shall be deemed prejudicial to the interests of their side.

That in consequence of the great abuse in the system of giving notes to excuse fagging, etc and otherwise exempt fellows from attendance at the matches, no notes shall be received which are not signed by one of the Medical Officers of the School, and countersigned by the Head of the House, or by a Master when the case specified is not illness.

That all fellows at Tutor during calling over, or otherwise absent, shall be obliged to attend as soon after as possible.

That the Head of the School take care that these resolutions be generally known among the School, and as far as the case may be they shall apply equally to the big sides.

That Old Rugbeians shall be allowed to play at the matches of Football, not without the consent, however, of the two heads of the sides.

Resolutions passed at the meeting which established the first Laws of the game.

Rules

1. FAIR CATCH, is a catch direct from the foot.

2. OFF SIDE. A player is off his side if the ball has touched one of his own side behind him, until the other side touch it.

3. FIRST OF HIS SIDE, is the player nearest the ball *on his side*.

4. A KNOCK ON, as distinguished from a *throw on*, consists in striking the ball on with the arm or hand.

5. TRY AT GOAL. A ball touched between the goalposts may be brought up to either of them, but not between. The ball when *punted* must be within, when caught without the line of goal: the ball must be place-kicked and not dropped, even though it touch two hands, and it must go over the bar and between the posts without having touched the dress or person of any player. No goal may be kicked from touch.

6. KICK OFF FROM MIDDLE must be a place.

7. KICK OUT must not be from more than ten yards out of goal of a place-kick, not more than twenty-five yards, if a punt, drop, or knock on.

8. RUNNING IN is allowed to any player on his side, provided he does not take the ball off the ground, or take it through touch.

9. CHARGING is fair, in case of a place-kick, as soon as a ball has touched the ground; in case of a kick from a catch, as soon as the player's foot has left the ground, and not before.

10. OFF SIDE. No player being off his side shall kick the ball in any case whatever.

11. No player being off his side shall hack, charge, run in, touch the ball in goal, or interrupt a catch.

12. A player when off his side, having a fair catch is entitled to a fair *knock on*, and in no other case.

13. A player being off his side shall not touch the ball on the ground, except in touch.

14. A player being off his side cannot put *on his side* himself, or any other player, by knocking or throwing on the ball.

15. TOUCH. A player may not in any case run with the ball in or through touch.

16. A player standing up to another may hold one arm only, but may hack him or knock the ball out of his hand if he attempt to kick it, or go beyond the line of touch.

17. An agreement between two players to send the ball *straight out* shall be allowed on big side.

18. A player having touched the ball straight for a tree, and touched the tree with it, may drop from either side if he can, but the opposite side may oblige him to go to his own side of the tree.

19. A player touching the ball off his side must *throw* it *straight out*.

20. All matches are drawn after five days, but after three if no goal has been kicked.

21. Two big side balls must always be in the Close during a match or big-side.

22. The discretion of sending into goals rests with the heads of sides or houses.

23. No football shall be played between the goals till the Sixth match.

24. Heads of sides, or two deputies appointed by them, are the sole arbiters of all disputes.

25. No strangers, in any match, may have a place kick at goal.

    a. Deputies may be allowed to act by the head of the School side, at the Sixth match.

26. No hacking with the heel, or above the knee, is fair.

27. No player but the first on his side, may be hacked, except in a *scrummage*.

28. No player may wear projecting nails or iron plates on the heels or soles of his shoes or boots.

29. No player may take the ball out of the Close.

30. No player may stop the ball with anything but his own person.

31. Nobody may wear cap or jersey without leave from the head of his house.

32. At a big-side, the two players highest in the School shall toss up.

33. The Island is all in goal.

34. At little sides the goals shall be four paces wide, and in kicking a goal the ball must pass out of the reach of any player present.

35. Three Praeposters constitute a big-side.

36. If a player take a punt when he is not entitled to it, the opposite side may take a punt or drop, without running if the ball has not touched two hands.

37. No player may be held, unless he is himself holding the ball.

As these rules have now become the Laws of the game, it is hoped that all who take an interest in Football will contribute all in their power to enforce their observance.

Interesting Anecdotes About the Game

From The New Rugbeian (1860)

"Fellows did not give a fig for the ball except in as much as it gave them a decent pretext for hacking. By jove, we'd been hacking for five minutes already and hadn't had half enough . . . My maxim is hack the ball on when you see it near you, and when you don't, why then hack the fellow next to you."

Rudyard Kipling

"Rugby Football is a game for muddied oafs"

Frederick Temple (headmaster 1858-69 and later Archbishop of Canterbury)

was once asked by a visitor with whom he was watching a game of football on the Close at Rugby, whether he, as a Headmaster would stop a game. 'Never', came the reply, 'short of manslaughter'.

Quote

"The sides were evenly matched, particularly in the Sixth match where about forty member of the Sixth faced four hundred and sixty, of whom two hundred stood forth to battle, Leaving the countless multitude to guard the camp.
The countless multitude were the fags who, in their everyday dress and top hats were sent to keep goal, whilst the older boys, resplendent in white trousers, emblazoned jerseys and velvet caps tasselled in silver and gold "followed up on the field of play."

"The Rugby Advertiser" January 28th 1871

Footballs "Our townsman Mr Gilbert, of St Matthews Street, has sent to Australia this week twenty dozens of his celebrated footballs as used at Rugby School."

The late Mr E.F. Bennett

writing to the "Morning Post" April 22nd 1930. "As I am more than eighty two years of age and my last football on Bigside (Rugby School Close) was in 1864, I can say something about the ball we used in those days, before the india rubber bladder had taken the place of animal bladders which James Gilbert used to blow tight with his great lungs.

The shape of the ball came from the bladder and was perfect shape for long distance kicking or placing and for dribbling too. The modern plum stone' is good for none of these, but seems meant for throwing or passing between players."

Rule 24 (of the 1846 codification)

A player having touched the ball straight for a tree and touched the tree with it, may drop from either side If he can, but one of the opposite side may oblige him to go to his own side of the tree."
The three famous elm trees on the Close in the middle of the 19th Century, were apparently part of the paraphernalia of the game. An interpretation of this rule seems to be that, if a player kicked the ball into the trees, he was entitled to a drop kick from either side of the trees. unless one of the opponents insisted that he take the kick from his own side of the trees.

The Sixth Match 1853 by W.D. Arnold

"It is a mild sunny day late in September, the grass is still green and untrodden, (for no football is allowed between the goals before the Sixth Match) the glorious elms have lost none of their rich verdure, the rooks, so characteristic of the Old Close, are cawing their enjoyment of the earliest illustrations of The Rugby Football Game."

How they scrummaged in the '80s
Sir J.H.A. McDonald
"Very few present had seen a real scrum. Had they ever seen a haycock that had been put up when the hay was wet and the smoke and steam was rising from it? That was just like a scrum in those days and it was just about as motionless."

Letter to "The Times" from 'A Surgeon'
Titley & McWhirter
In this letter the surgeon gives a list of injuries he has attended at Rugby School Matches, "one boy with his collar bone broken, another with a severe injury to the ankle, a third with a severe injury to the knee and two others sent home on crutches."

An early game on the close. Note the great number of players and size and shape of the ball.

Alouette

Traditional

♩=132 **CHORUS**

Al - ou-et - te, gen-tille Al - ou-et - te.

Al - ou-et - te, je te plum-er - ai. 1.Oh, I

love her chees-y flaps, Oh, I love her chees-y flaps.

Repeat this bar as necessary

D.C. al Fine

Chees-y flaps, chees-y flaps. Al - ou-ette, Al - ou-ette. Oh.

2. Oh, I love her slippery slit,
   Oh, I love her slippery slit.
   Slippery slit, slippery slit.
   Cheesy flaps, cheesy flaps.
   Alouette, Alouette. Oh.
   CHORUS

3. O, I love her pinky nips,...
   CHORUS

4. Oh, I love her throbbing thighs,...
   CHORUS

As I Was Walking

Traditional

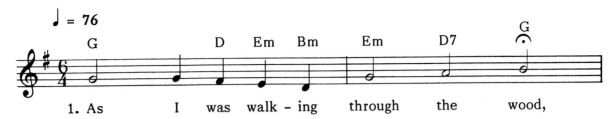

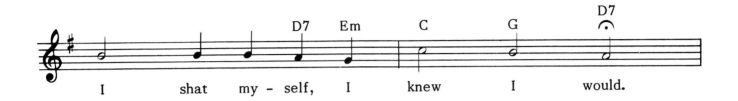

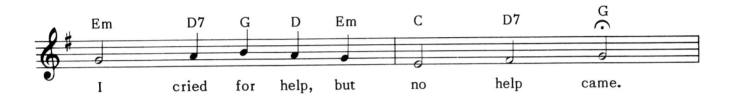

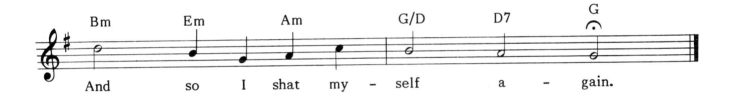

2. As I was walking through the hall,

   Some nancy grabbed me by the balls.

   I cried for help, but no help came

   And so he grabbed my balls again.

3. As I was walking through a gate,

   I was accosted by a saint.

   I cried for help, but no help came

   And so he grabbed my balls again.

The Alphabet

Traditional

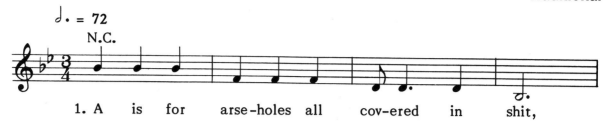

1. A is for arse-holes all cov-ered in shit, "Hey ho," said Ro - ly; ——— And

B is for bug - ger that rev-els in it With a

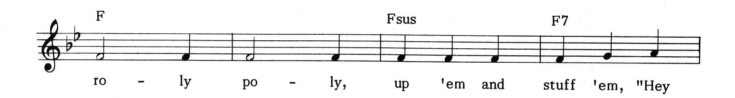

ro - ly po - ly, up 'em and stuff 'em, "Hey

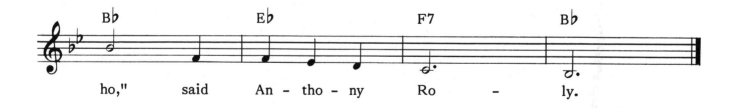

ho," said An - tho - ny Ro - ly.

2. C is for cunt, all dripping with piss,
   "Hey ho," said Roly;
   And D is for drunkard who gave it a kiss
   With a roly poly, . . .

3. E is for eunuch with only one ball,
   "Hey ho," said Roly;
   And F for the fucker with no balls at all
   With a roly poly, . . .

4. G is for gonorrhoea, goitre and gout,
   "Hey ho," said Roly;
   And H is for harlot that spreads it about
   With a roly poly, . . .

5. I is injection for syphilis and itch,
   "Hey ho," said Roly;
   And J is for jerk of a dog on a bitch
   With a roly poly, . . .

6. K is for kiss the virgin thought nice,
   "Hey ho," said Roly;
   And L is for lecher who stuffs it in twice
   With a roly poly, . . .

7. M is for monk - the dirty old sod,
   "Hey ho," said Roly;
   And N is for nun what he put in the pod
   With a roly poly, . . .

8. O is for orifice now fully revealed,
   "Hey ho," said Roly;
   And P is for penis with foreskin back-peeled
   With a roly poly, . . .

9. Q is for quaker that shat in his hat,
   "Hey ho," said Roly;
   And R is for Roger who rogered the cat
   With a roly poly, . . .

10. S is for shit-pot all full to the brim,
    "Hey ho," said Roly;
    And T is for turds that are floating therein
    With a roly poly, . . .

11. U is for usher who pulled on his pod,
    "Hey ho," said Roly;
    And V is for virgin who wished that she could
    With a roly poly, . . .

12. W's for whore whose fucking's a farce,
    "Hey ho," said Roly;
    And X, Y and Z you can shove up your arse
    With a roly poly, . . .

Aunty Mary

Traditional

Aunt - ie Ma - ry had a can-ar - y up the leg of her

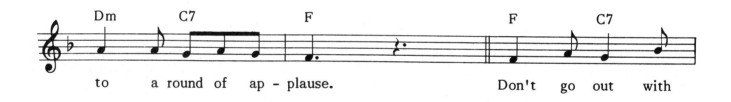

draws; When she fart - ed it de-part - ed

to a round of ap - plause. Don't go out with

girls an - y more, don't go out with Ma - ry;

Don't go out with girls an-y more, oops! I'm a fai - ry.

British Gonorrhoea

Traditional

1.Some die from drink-ing whisk- y and—some from drink—ing—beer. Some

die of con - sti - pa - tion and— some of di— arr— hoea. A—

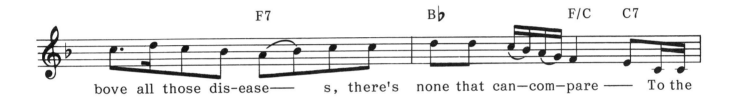

bove all those dis-ease—— s, there's none that can—com-pare —— To the

drip, drip, drip of a syphil-it - ic prick And they call it gon— orr— hoea.

2. I like the girls who say they will,
    I like the girls who won't.
    I don't like girls who say they will
    And then they say they won't.
    But of all the girls I like the best,
    It may be wrong or right;
    Are the girls who say they never will
    And look as though they might.

Cats On The Rooftops

Traditional

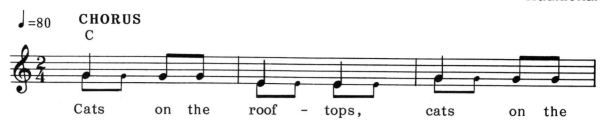

Cats on the roof - tops, cats on the tiles, Cats with the clap and cats with

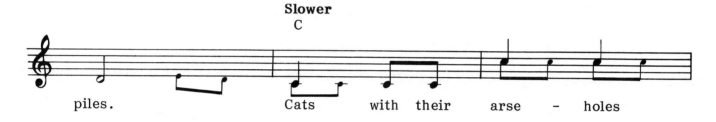

piles. Cats with their arse - holes

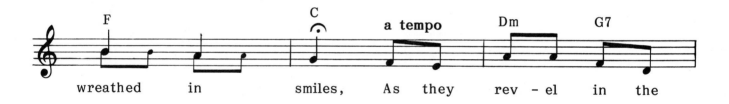

wreathed in smiles, As they rev - el in the

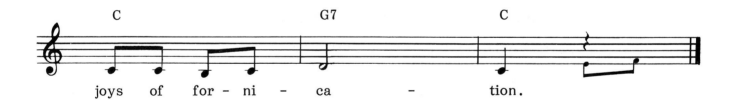

joys of for - ni - ca - tion.

2. If you wake up in the morning with a devil of a stand,
   From the pressure of the fluid on the semenary gland;
   If you haven't got a woman use your own horny hand,
   As you revel in the joys of masturbation.
   CHORUS

3. The regimental Sergeant Major leads a lonely life,

'Cause he hasn't got a mistress and he hasn't got a wife;

So he sticks it up the arsehole of the regimental fife,

As he revels in the joys of fornication.

CHORUS

4. Long legged curates, pride like goats;

Pale faced spinsters shag like stoats.

The whole damn world stands by and gloats,

As they revel in the joys of fornication.

CHORUS

5. The ostrich in the desert is a solitary chick,

Without the opportunity to dip its wick;

But when he does, it slips in thick,

As he revels in the joys of fornication.

CHORUS

The Chandler's Boy

Traditional

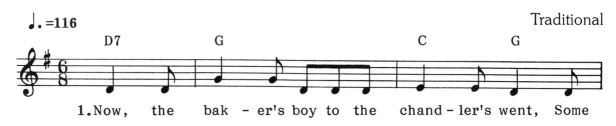

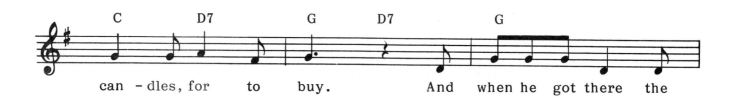

1.Now, the bak - er's boy to the chand - ler's went, Some

can - dles, for to buy. And when he got there the

place was bare, No - one, could he es - py. And

just as he was a - bout to leave, Think-ing the place was

dead, He heard the sound of a rub-be-di-dub

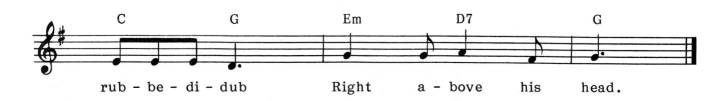

Right a-bove his head. Oh, he heard the sound of a

rub-be-di-dub Right a - bove his head.

2. Oh, the baker's boy was cunning and wise,
   And he crept up the stairs.
   He crept up there so silently,
   He caught them unaware.
   And then he saw the butcher's boy
   Between the mistress' thighs;
   And they were having a rub-be-di-dub,
   Right before his eyes.
   Oh,...

3. Now, the mistress, she was most alarmed
   She jumped right off the bed.
   She rushed up to the baker's boy
   And this is what she said;
   "If you will but my secret keep,
   You can bear this fact in mind -
   You can always have a rub-be-di-dub,
   Whenever you feel inclined!"
   Oh,...

4. Now, the baker's boy filled with joy
   At the prospect of such fun.
   He vowed he leap upon the bed
   When the butcher's boy was done.
   And as he came to the shorter strokes
   And kissed the Chandler's wife,
   He vowed he'd have a rub-be-di-dub,
   Every day of his life.
   Oh,...

5. But, in the morn when he awoke,
   All over, did he shake.
   His back was raw,
   His balls were sore
   All over, did he ache.
   And when he looked at his john-tom,
   He saw he'd done the trick;
   The consequence of his rub-be-di-dub
   Was pimples on his prick.
   Oh,...

6. Now, the baker's boy to doctor's went,
   Appointment for to buy.
   The doctor looked him up and down
   And heaved a mighty sigh.
   "My son, my son, my son!" he said,
   "You've been a bloody fool -
   You'll never more have a rub-be-di-dub
   I'm gonna cut off your tool!"
   Oh,...

7. So, listen to the baker's boy,
   For he should surely know;
   An enthusiastic amateur,
   Is worse than any pro'.
   So, if you must a wooing go
   And self control you lack;
   Then, whenever you have a rub-be-di-dub,
   Be sure to wear a mac.
   Oh,...

The Cowpuncher's Whore

Traditional

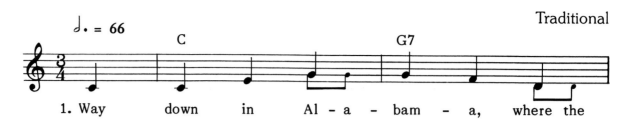

1. Way down in Al - a - bam - a, where the

bull - shit lies thick, The girls are so pret - ty, the

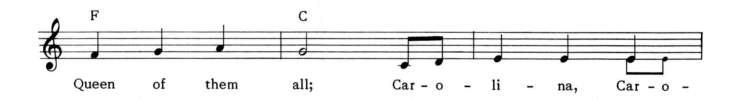

ba - bies come quick. You'll find Car - o - li - na's the

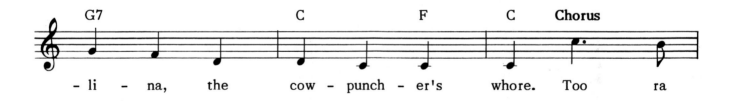

Queen of them all; Car - o - li - na, Car - o -

- li - na, the cow - punch - er's whore. Too ra

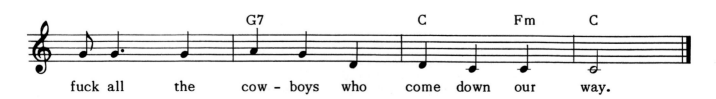

loo, ——————— too ra lay, ——————— And we'll

fuck all the cow - boys who come down our way.

2. She's handy, she's randy, she shags on the street.
   Whenever you meet her, she's always on heat.
   If you leave your flies open, she's after your meat,
   And the smell of her cunt knocks you right off your feet.

   CHORUS

3. One day I was riding way down by the falls,
   One hand on my pistol, one hand on my balls,
   I spied Carolina a-using a stick,
   Instead of the end of the cow-puncher's prick.

   CHORUS

4. I caressed her, undressed her and laid her down there,
   And parted the trusses of curly brown hair,
   Inserted the penis of my trusty horse
   And then there began such a strange intercourse.

   CHORUS

5. Faster and faster went my trusty steed,
   Until Carolina rejoiced at the speed.
   All of a sudden, my horse did backfire
   And shot Carolina right into the mire.

   CHORUS

6. Up got Carolina, all covered in muck
   And said, "Oh my God, what a glorious fuck!"
   Took two paces forward and fell to the floor,
   And that was the end of the cow-puncher's whore.

   CHORUS

The Cuckoo

Traditional

1. The cuck-oo is a fun-ny bird; it— sits in the grass, With its wings neat - ly fold - ed and its

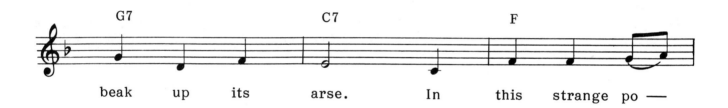

beak up its arse. In this strange po —

si - tion it — just says "twit twit," 'Cause it's

hard to say "cuck-oo" with a beak full of shit.

Darkie Sunday School

Traditional

Chorus: Young folk, old folk, ev - 'ry-bo - dy come

To the dark - ie Sun - day School and we'll have lots of fun.

Bring your sticks of chew - ing gum and sit up - on the floor, We'll

tell you bi - ble stor - ies that you've nev - er heard be-fore.

1. Adam was the first man, so we're led to believe;
   He walked into the garden and bumped right into Eve.
   There was no one to show him - he quickly found a way;
   And that's the merry reason we're singing here today.

   CHORUS

2. The Lord said unto Noah, "It's going to rain today."
   So, Noah built a bloody great ark in which to sail away.
   The animals went in two by two, but soon got up to tricks;
   Although they went in two by two, they came out six by six.

   CHORUS

3. Moses in the bulrushes was all wrapped up in suede;
   The Pharaoh's daughter found him and then began to bathe
   She took him back to Pharaoh and said, "I'm unsure;"
   And Pharaoh winked his eye and said, "I've never done that before."

   CHORUS

4. Samson was an Israelite and very big and strong,
   Delilah was a Philistine, always doing wrong.
   They spent a week together - It didn't get very hot;
   For all he got was short back and sides, and a little bit off the top.

   CHORUS

Dinah, Dinah

Traditional

CHORUS: Di - nah, Di - nah show us your leg, Show us your leg, show us your leg. Di - nah, Di - nah show us your leg a yard a - bove your knee. 1. A knee.

1. A rich girl has a limousine,
    A poor girl has a truck;
    But the only time that Dinah rides
    Is when she has a fuck.
    CHORUS

2. A rich girl has a brassiere,
    A poor girl uses string;
    But Dinah uses nothing at all -
    She lets the bastards swing.
    CHORUS

3. A rich girl has a ring of gold,
    A poor girl one of brass;
    But the only ring that Dinah has
    Is the one around her arse.
    CHORUS

4. A rich girl uses vaseline,
    A poor girl uses lard;
    But Dinah uses axle grease
    Because her cunt's so hard.
    CHORUS

5. A rich girl uses sanitary towels,
    A poor girl uses sheets;
    But Dinah uses nothing at all -
    See the trail along the streets.
    CHORUS

The Farmer's Boy

Traditional

* Blow a raspberry

** Repeat these bars, in reverse order, as necessary

Four And Twenty Virgins

Traditional

♩ = 126

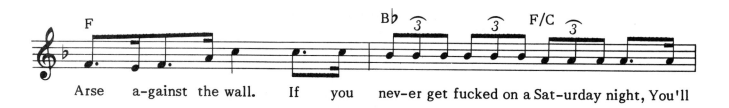

1. Four and twen-ty vir - gins Came down from In - ver-ness.

When the war was over, There were four and twenty less. Sing-ing balls to your fath-er,

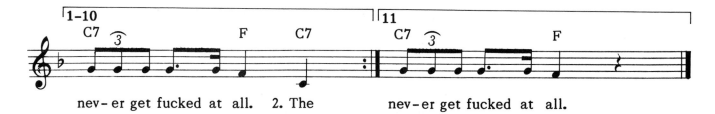

Arse a-gainst the wall. If you nev-er get fucked on a Sat-urday night, You'll

1–10
nev-er get fucked at all. 2. The

11
nev-er get fucked at all.

2. The village parson, he was there,
   Sitting by the fire,
   Knitting rubber johnnies
   From an old dunlop tyre.

   CHORUS

3. The village virgin, she was there,
   Sitting at the front;
   Broken glass around her arse,
   Barbed wire around her cunt.

   CHORUS

4. The village cripple, he was there,
   He wasn't up to much;
   Lining the girls against the wall
   And fucking them with his crutch.

   CHORUS

5. The village teacher, she was there,
   Sitting with her class;
   Stroking all the little boys
   And taking it up her ass.

   CHORUS

6. The village postman, he was there,
   He had a dose of pox.
   So, instead of screwing women,
   He screwed the letterbox.

   CHORUS

7. The vicar's daughter, she was there,
   Up to her usual tricks;
   Jumping off the mantlepiece
   And landing on her tits.

   CHORUS

8. The village idiot, he was there,
   Sitting on a pole,
   Pulling his foreskin over his head
   And whistling through the hole.

   CHORUS

9. The village maid, she was there,
   Explaining to the groom
   That the vagina, not the rectum,
   Was the entrance to the womb.

   CHORUS

10. The village bobby, he was there;
    Pride of all the force.
    They found him in the stables,
    Wanking off a horse.

    CHORUS

11. The village farmer, he was there,
    He'd on our fancy socks.
    He fucked a lassie forty times,
    Then found she had the pox.

    CHORUS

The Foreskin Fusiliers

Traditional

Eyes right, skins back tight. Chop-pers to the

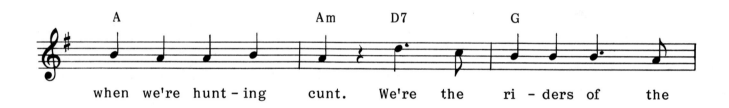

fore. We're the boys that make no noise,

when we're hunt-ing cunt. We're the ri-ders of the

night; we'd ra-ther fuck than fight. We're the

boys of the fore-skin fu-si-liers.———

A French Man Went To The Lavatory

Traditional

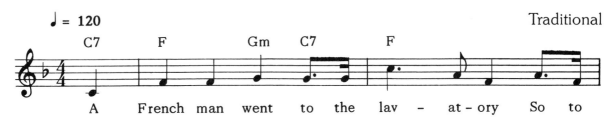

A French man went to the lav – at-ory So to

have a jol-ly good shit. He took his coat and his

trous – ers off So that he could rev-el in it. But —

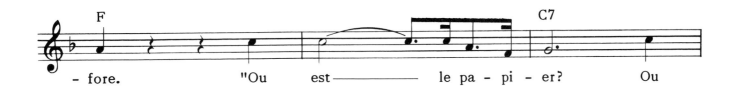

– fore. "Ou est —— le pa – pi – er? Ou

est —— le pa – pi – er? J'as – sure, mon – sieur,

Je fais man – ure; Ou est —— le pa – pi – er?"

Gentlemen, Should Please Refrain

Traditional

1. Once the train is in the sta - tion, please refrain from ur - in - a - tion -

Have re-gard for rail - way prop - er - ty.

If you want to pass some wa - ter, go and ask a rail - way port - er -

He will show you to the lav - a - tory.

2. If the train is stationary and you want to go quite heavy,

Do not drop your lot into the train.

From the carriage you must wander and a penny you must squander

And relieve yourself with might and may.

I Don't Want To Join The Army

Traditional

VERSE

Monday night I touched her on the ankle,
Tuesday I touched her on the knee.
On Wednesday night, success! I lifted up her dress,
Thursday night well, oh! cor blimey.
Friday night I had my hand upon it,
Saturday night she gave my balls a tweak.
On Sunday after supper,
I rammed the fucker up her,
And now I'm paying seventy bob a week. Cor blimey.

CHORUS

© 1991 International Music Publications

The Hole In The Elephant's Bottom

Traditional

1. My am - bi-tions to go on the stage; —— And from

this you can see that I've got 'em.—— In pan-to-mimes I'm all ar -

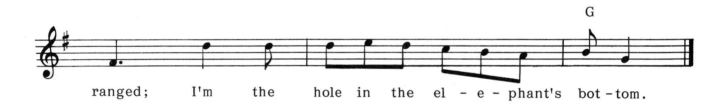

ranged; I'm the hole in the el - e - phant's bot -tom.

2. And the girls all around think I'm it;

   As they sit in the stalls I can spot 'em.

   And I wink at the girls in the pit

   Through the hole in the elephant's bottom.

3. One night we performed in a farce,

   And they stuffed up the bottom with cotton.

   But it split and I showed my bare arse

   Through the hole in the elephant's bottom.

4. There are pockets inside in the cloth,

   For two bottles of "Bass", if you've got 'em.

   But they hiss and they boom so I blow out the froth

   Through the hole in the elephant's bottom.

5. Now, my part hasn't got any worse,

   But there's nothing that can't be forgotten.

   I spend all my time pushing copular turds

   Through the hole in the elephant's bottom.

6. Some may think this story is good

   And some may believe that it's rotten.

   But those that don't like it can stuff it right up

   The hole in the elephant's bottom.

I Haven't Seen Old Hitler

♩=120

Traditional

Oh, I have-n't seen old Hit-ler for a hell of a time. I

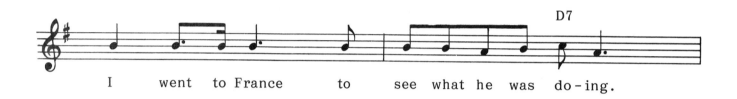

have-n't seen old Hit-ler for a hell of a time.

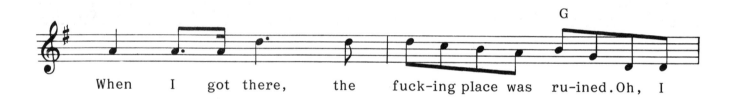

I went to France to see what he was do-ing.

When I got there, the fuck-ing place was ru-ined. Oh, I

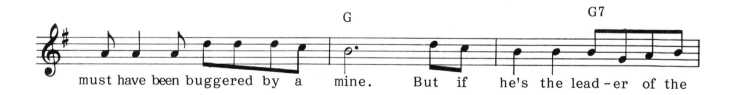

have-n't seen old Hit-ler for a hell of a time. He

must have been buggered by a mine. But if he's the lead-er of the

Deutch-land breed-er, Fuck him! He's no cou-sin of mine. No

cou-sin of mine, no cou-sin of mine. I've got cou-sins of

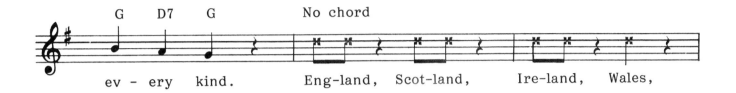

ev - ery kind. Eng-land, Scot-land, Ire-land, Wales,

Rus - sia, Prus - sia and Jer - u - sa - lem,

Af - ri - ca, Am - er - i - ca and Ger - man - y

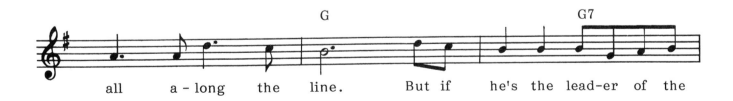

all a - long the line. But if he's the lead-er of the

Deutch-land breed- er, Fuck him! He's no cou-sin of mine.

I Used To Work In Chicago

Traditional

Oh, I used to work in Chi - ca - go in an

old de-part - ment store, I used to work in Chi -

ca - go but I don't work there an - y more. 1. A

wo-man came in for some car - pets, Car-pets from the store;

Carpets she want-ed, layed she got and I don't work there an-y more.

2. A woman came in for some nails,
Nails from the store.
Nails she wanted, screwed she got
And I don't work there any more.
CHORUS

3. A woman came in for some tobacco,
Tobacco from the store.
Tobacco she wanted, shagged she got
And I don't work there any more.
CHORUS

4. A woman came in for some apples,
   Apples from the store.
   Apples she wanted, crabs she got
   And I don't work there any more.
   CHORUS

5. A woman came in for some chicken,
   Chicken from the store.
   Chicken she wanted, cock she got
   And I don't work there any more.
   CHORUS

6. A woman came in for some butter,
   Butter from the store.
   Butter she wanted, stork she got
   And I don't work there any more.
   CHORUS

7. A woman came in for some turkey,
   Turkey from the store.
   Turkey she wanted, gobble she got
   And I don't work there any more.
   CHORUS

8. A woman came in for some vegetables,
   Vegetables from the store.
   Vegetables she wanted, root she got
   And I don't work there any more.
   CHORUS

9. A woman came in for bananas,
   Bananas from the store.
   Bananas she wanted, skin she got
   And I don't work there any more.
   CHORUS

10. A woman came in for some needles,
    Needles from the store.
    Needles she wanted, prick she got
    And I don't work there any more.
    CHORUS

If I Were The Marrying Kind

Traditional

1. If I were the mar-ry-ing kind, And thank the Lord I'm

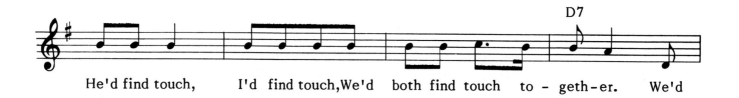

not, sir; The kind of man that I would wed would be a rug - by full-back.

He'd find touch, I'd find touch, We'd both find touch to - geth - er. We'd

be al-right in the mid-dle of the night, Find - ing touch to - geth - er.

2. If I were the marrying kind,
   And thank the Lord I'm not, sir;
   The Kind of man that I would wed
   Would be a wing three quarter.
   He'd go hard, I'd go hard,
   We'd both go hard together.
   We'd be alright in the middle of the night,
   Going hard together.

3. If I were the marrying kind,
   And thank the Lord I'm not, sir;
   The kind of man that I would wed
   Would be a centre quarter.
   He'd pass out, I'd pass out,
   We'd both pass out together.
   We'd be alright in the middle of the night,
   Passing out together.

4. If I were the marrying kind,
   And thank the Lord I'm not, sir;
   The kind of man that I would wed
   Would be rugby fly half.
   He'd whip it out, I'd whip it out,
   We'd both whip it out together.
   We'd be alright in the middle of the night,
   Whipping it out together.

5. If I were the marrying kind,
   And thank the Lord I'm not, sir;
   The kind of man that I would wed
   Would be a rugby scrum half.
   He'd put it in, I'd put it in,
   We'd both put it in together.
   We'd be alright in the middle of the night,
   Putting it in together.

6. If I were the marrying kind,
   And thank the Lord I'm not, sir;
   The kind of man that I would wed
   Would be a rugby hooker.
   He'd strike hard, I'd strike hard,
   We'd both strike hard together.
   We'd be alright in the middle of the night,
   Striking hard together.

7. If I were the marrying kind,
   And thank the Lord I'm not, sir;
   The kind of man that I would wed
   Would be a referee.
   He would blow, I would blow,
   We'd both blow hard together.
   We'd be alright in the middle of the night,
   Blowing hard together.

In Mobile

♩ = 132

Traditional

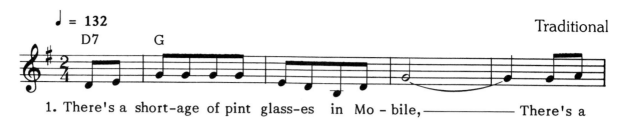

1. There's a short-age of pint glass-es in Mo - bile, ————— There's a

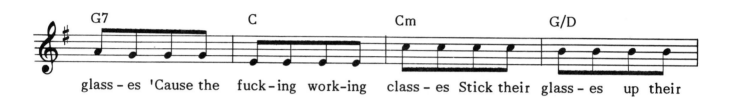

short-age of pint glass-es in Mo - bile, ————— There's a short-age of pint

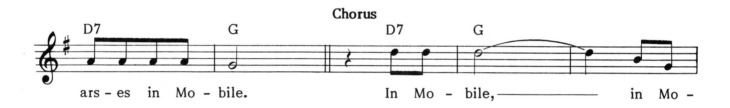

glass - es 'Cause the fuck-ing work-ing class - es Stick their glass - es up their

Chorus

ars - es in Mo - bile. In Mo - bile, ————— in Mo -

- bile, ————— In Mo in Mo in Mo in Mo - bile —————

————— There's a short-age of pint glass-es 'cause the fuck-ing work-ing

class - es Stick their glass-es up their ars - es in Mo - bile.—————

2. There's a man called Johnny Hunt in Mobile,
There's a man called Johnny Hunt in Mobile,
There's a man called Johnny Hunt
And he thought he had a cunt,
'Cause his arse was back to front in Mobile.

CHORUS

3. Oh the eagles, they fly high in Mobile,
Oh the eagles, they fly high in Mobile,
Oh the eagles, they fly high
And they crap right in your eye,
Oh, I'm glad that cats don't fly in Mobile.

CHORUS

4. There's a shortage of good bogs in Mobile,
There's a shortage of good bogs in Mobile,
There's a shortage of good bogs
So they wait until it clogs,
Then they chop it into logs in Mobile.

CHORUS

5. In the bogs there is no paper in Mobile,
In the bogs there is no paper in Mobile,
In the bogs there is no paper
So they wait until it's vapour,
Then they light it with a taper in Mobile.

CHORUS

6. Oh the vicar is a bugger in Mobile,
Oh the vicar is a bugger in Mobile,
Oh the vicar is a bugger
And the curate is another,
So they bugger one another in Mobile.

CHORUS

7. Oh there was a man called Best in Mobile,
Oh there was a man called Best in Mobile,
Oh there was a man called Best
And he thought he had a breast,
But his balls were on his chest in Mobile.

CHORUS

8. Oh there was a man called Frank in Mobile,
Oh there was a man called Frank in Mobile,
Oh there was a man called Frank
And they tied him to a plank,
So he couldn't have a *scratch* in Mobile.

CHORUS

The Jolly Tinker

♩ = 112

Traditional

1. Now, the la - dy of the nab - ob Was dress - ing for the

ball, When she spied a jol - ly tin - ker piss - ing up a - gainst the

wall. With his blood-y great kid - ney wip - er and his

balls the size of three, And a yard and a half of

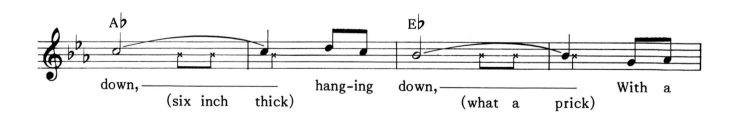

fore - skin hang - ing down be-low his knee. Hang - ing

down, ——————— hang-ing down, ——————— With a
(six inch thick) (what a prick)

yard and a half of fore - skin hang-ing down be-low his knee.

2. Well, she wrote to him a letter
   And in it she did write:
   Well, I'd rather be fucked by you sir,
   Than his lordship any night.

   CHORUS

3. Well now, he received this letter
   When he was having tea,
   And he overturned the table
   With a stand of four foot three.

   CHORUS

4. Well, he jumped upon his charger
   And away he did ride,
   With his balls slung over his shoulder
   And his penis by his side.

   CHORUS

5. Well, he rode up to the menhir,
   He rode up to the hall.
   "Oh, God save us!" said the butler
   " 'Cause he's come to fuck us all!"

   CHORUS

6. There was fucking in the parlour,
   There was fucking in the hall.
   But the tiny fuck, the butler,
   Was the funniest fuck of all.

   CHORUS

7. Now, some say he went to heaven,
   Some say he went to hell,
   And some say he fucked the devil
   And he fucked him fucking well.

   CHORUS

Large Balls

Traditional

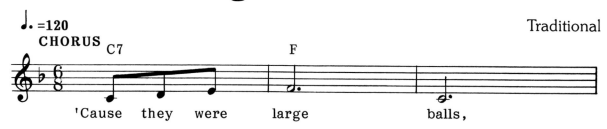

'Cause they were large balls,

balls as heav-y as lead. With a dex-ter-ous twist of his

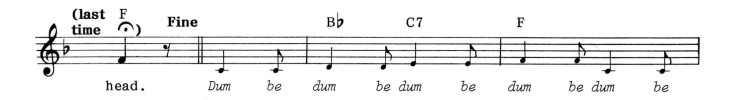

mus - cu - lar wrist he could flick 'em right o - ver his

head. *Dum be dum be dum be dum be dum be*

dum be. 1.Now, there was a man called An-tho-ny Clare -

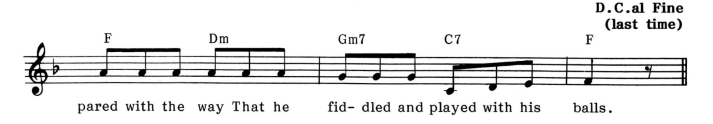

He was a ve-ry fine jug - ul-aire; There was-n't a man who com -

pared with the way That he fid- dled and played with his balls.

2. Now, Anthony walking down the street –
   Just by chance he happened to meet
   A pretty young maid with a dog at her feet,
   Watching him play with his balls.
   CHORUS

3. Now, Anthony swung them round and round,
   And let them go with a hell of a bound,
   Right on the head of the faithful hound
   That was watching him play with his balls.
   CHORUS

4. Now, the maiden, she was overawed –
   Swore she's take the case to court
   For in her opinion, no man aught
   To be twisting and playing with his balls.
   CHORUS

5. They took him to a magistrate
   Who put him in a cell in slate,
   And left him there to meditate
   And fiddle, and play with his balls.
   CHORUS

6. And when they took the case to court,
   The lawyer of the lady sought
   To prove that Anthony didn't aught
   To twist and play with his balls.
   CHORUS

7. The jury said, "It's a bloody disgrace,
   Exposing yourself in a public place,
   Waggling your tool in a lady's face,
   Twisting and playing with your balls!"
   CHORUS

8. The judge and jury couldn't agree
   And the judge, he said, "It's plain to see,
   And really and truly, I cannot see why
   A man shouldn't play with his balls."
   CHORUS

9. Then Anthony gave the court a shock;
   As bold as brass, he left the dock,
   Swinging his balls around his cock,
   Twisting and playing with his balls.
   CHORUS

10. And here is the moral of this song –
    If you play with your balls, you can't go wrong,
    So, bang your cock against the gong,
    Then fiddle and play with your balls.
    CHORUS

Life Presents A Dismal Picture

Traditional

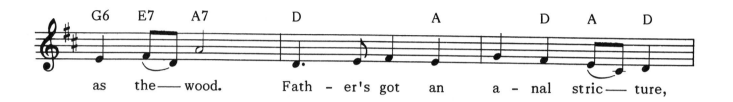

1. Life presents a dis - mal pic——ture, Dark and drear - y,

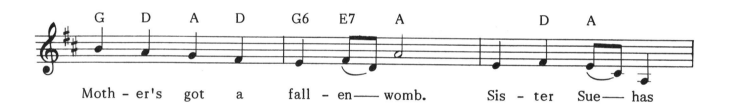

as the——wood. Fath - er's got an a - nal stric——ture,

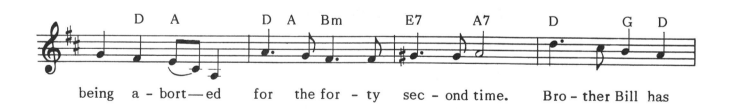

Moth - er's got a fall - en——womb. Sis - ter Sue——has

being a - bort——ed for the for - ty sec - ond time. Bro - ther Bill has

being de - port——ed for a——ho - mo——sex - ual——crime.

2. Nurse has got her menstruation –

   Never laughs and never smiles.

   Life's a dismal occupation

   Cracking ice for Grandpa's piles.

   In a small brown paper parcel,

   Wrapped in a mysterious way,

   Is an imitation rectum;

   Grant and use it twice a day.

3. Joe the postman called this morning,

   Stuck his penis through the door.

   We could not, despite endearment,

   Get it out 'til half past four.

   Even now, the baby's started

   Having epileptic fits.

   Every time it coughs, it spews;

   Every time it laughs, it shits.

3. Yet we are not broken hearted,

   Neither are we up the spout.

   Auntie Mabel has just farted –

   Blown her arsehole inside out.

   Life presents a dismal picture,

   Dark and dreary, as the wood.

   Father's got an anal stricture,

   Mother's got a fallen womb.

The Lobster Song

Traditional

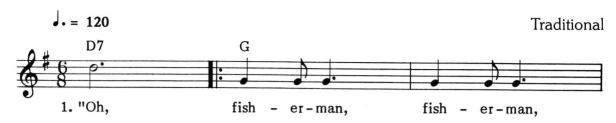

1. "Oh, fish - er - man, fish - er - man,

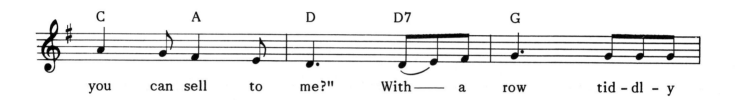

home from the sea, Have you got a lob - ster

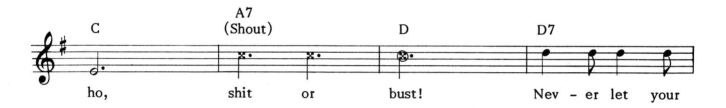

you can sell to me?" With—— a row tid - dl - y

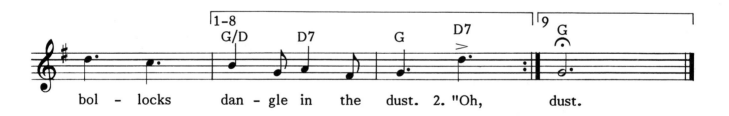

ho, shit or bust! Nev - er let your

bol - locks dan - gle in the dust. 2. "Oh, dust.

2. "Oh, yes sir, yes sir, I have two

And the biggest of the bastards I will sell to you."

With a . . .

3. I took the lobster home but I couldn't find a dish,

So I put it in the place where the missus has a piss.

With a . . .

© 1991 International Music Publications

4. Early in the morning, as you all know;

♪ │ ♩. ♩ ♪ │

The missus got up to let the water flow,

With a . . .

5. First there was a yell and then there came a crunch,

Then out came the missus with a lobster up her cunt.

With a . . .

6. Well, the missus grabbed a brush and I grabbed a broom,

And we chased the fucking lobster round and round the room.

With a . . .

7. Oh, we hit it on the head and we hit it on the side,

Yes, we hit the fucking lobster until it nearly died.

With a . . .

8. Oh, this story has a moral and the moral is this;

Always have a 'shifty' before you have a piss.

With a . . .

9. This is the ending - if you should ask for more,

There's an apple up my arse-hole and you can have the core.

With a . . .

Maggie May

Traditional

Chorus: Oh, Mag-gie, Mag-gie May, they have tak-en her a-way And she'll

nev-er walk a back street an-y more. You dirt-y rotten scrounger, you

ran it home and had her. You dirt-y rob-bing bast-ard, Mag-gie May.

1. Oh, the night that Maggie died, she pulled me to her side

And bequeathed me with a pair of flannel draws.

They were tattered, they were torn,

Round the arsehole they were worn;

They're the only flannel draws that Maggie wore.

CHORUS

Matilda

Traditional

Mary In The Kitchen

Traditional

♩ = 92

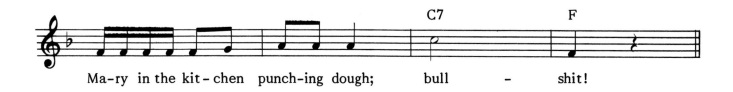

1. Ma-ry in the kit-chen punching dough,   punching dough,   punching dough,

Ma-ry in the kit-chen   punch-ing dough;   bull   -   shit!

Ma-ry in the kit-chen punching dough When the cheeks of her arse went chuff,chuff,chuff.

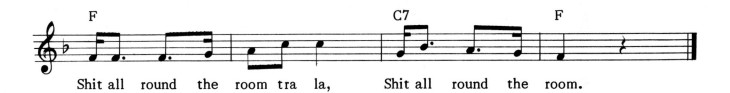

Shit all   round   the   room tra la,   Shit all   round   the   room.

2. Mary in the kitchen boiling rice, boiling rice, boiling rice.

Mary in the kitchen boiling rice; bullshit!

Mary in the kitchen boiling rice

While the lips of her cunt sing, "Three blind mice."

Shit all round the room tra la, shit all round the room.

3. Mary in the kitchen shelling peas, shelling peas, shelling peas.

   Mary in the kitchen shelling peas; bullshit!

   Mary in the kitchen shelling peas

   While the hairs round her cunt hang down to her knees.

   Shit all round the room tra la, shit all round the room.

4. Mary in the garden sifting cinders, sifting cinders, sifting cinders.

   Mary in the garden sifting cinders; bullshit!

   Mary in the garden sifting cinders,

   Blew one fart and broke ten windows.

   Shit all round the room tra la, shit all round the room.

5. Mary had a dog whose name was Ben, name was Ben, name was Ben.

   Mary had a dog whose name was Ben; bullshit!

   Mary had a dog whose name was Ben,

   He had one cock but screwed like ten.

   Shit all round the room tra la, shit all round the room.

6. Mary in the kitchen baking cakes, baking cakes, baking cakes,

   Mary in the kitchen baking cakes; bullshit!

   Mary in the kitchen baking cakes

   When out from her tits came two milkshakes.

   Shit all round the room tra la, shit all round the room.

The Money Rolls In

Traditional

1. My fath-er makes books on the corn-er, —— My

moth-er makes int'-rest-ing gin, —— My sis-ter sells kiss-es to

sail-ors; —— My God, how the mon-ey rolls in. Rolls in,

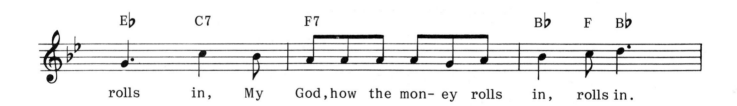

rolls in, My God, how the mon-ey rolls in, rolls in.

Rolls in, rolls in, My God, how the mon-ey rolls in.

2. My sister's a barmaid in Sydney,

For a shilling, she'll strip to the skin.

She's dripping from morning to midnight;

My God, how the money rolls in.

CHORUS

3. My mother's a bonny housekeeper,

   Every night when the evening grows dim,

   She hangs out her little red lantern;

   My God, how the money rolls in.

   CHORUS

4. My cousin's a Harley Street surgeon,

   With instruments long, sharp and thin.

   He only does one operation;

   My God, how the money rolls in.

   CHORUS

5. Joe is a registered plumber

   His business is awfully thin.

   He'll plug your old hole for a tenner;

   My God, how the money rolls in.

   CHORUS

6. My brother's a poor missionary,

   He saves all the women from sin.

   He'll save you a pound for a penny;

   My God, how the money rolls in.

   CHORUS

7. I've lost all my cash on the horses,

   I'm sick from my interest in gin;

   I'm falling in love with my mother;

   My God, what a mess I am in!

   CHORUS

No Balls At All

Traditional

1. How well she re - mem - bers the

night she was wed; She pulled back the

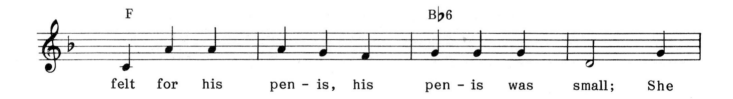

cov - ers and jumped in - to bed. She

felt for his pen - is, his pen - is was small; She

felt for his balls, he had no balls at

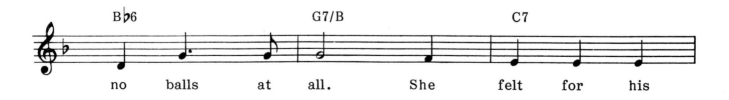

all. What?! No balls at all,

no balls at all. She felt for his

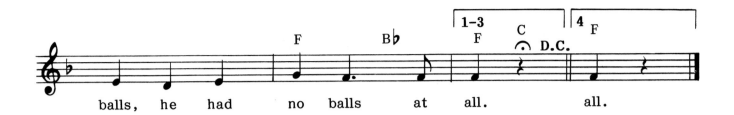

balls,   he   had   no   balls   at   all.   all.

2. Oh mummy, oh mummy, oh, what can I do?
   I've married this lad who's unable to screw.
   I felt for his penis, his penis was small;
   I felt for his balls, he had no balls at all.
   CHORUS

3. Oh daughter, oh daughter, oh, don't be so sad,
   The very same trouble I had with your dad.
   But many a lad will answer the call
   Of a wife with a husband with no balls at all.
   CHORUS

4. Now, this little girlie took mummies advice
   And found the procedure exceedingly nice;
   A bonny, fat baby was born in the hall,
   But the poor little bastard had no balls at all.
   CHORUS

Oh Dear, What Can The Matter Be?

Traditional

♩. = 60

Oh dear, what can the mat-ter be? Sev-en old lad-ies

locked in a lav-a-tory. They were there from Sun-day to Sat-ur-day –

No-bo-dy knew they were there.— 1. They said they were go-ing to

chat to the Vi-car; They went in to-geth-er, they thought it was quick-er. The

lav-a-tory door was a bit of a sticker, And the Vic-ar had tea all a-lone.

2. The first was a wife of a deacon in Dover
   And though she was known as a bit of a rover,
   She liked it so much she thought she'd got turned over
   And nobody knew she was there.

CHORUS

3. The next dear lady was old Miss Bickles;
   She found herself in a desperate pickle,
   She shouted at Mabel she hadn't a nickle
   And nobody knew she was there.

   CHORUS

4. The next was the Bishop of Chichester's daughter
   Who went to the parson's to help her pass water
   She pulled on the chain and the writings I caught her
   And nobody knew she was there.

   CHORUS

5. The next old lady was Abergail Humphrey,
   Who settled inside to make herself comfy;
   And then she found out she could not get her bum free,
   And nobody knew she was there.

   CHORUS

6. The next old lady was Elizabeth Spender
   Who's doing alright 'til her vagrant suspender
   Got all twisted up in her feminine gender,
   And nobody knew she was there.

   CHORUS

7. The last was a lady named Jennifer Trip,
   She only sat down on her personal whip.
   But now she's got quim streaks that cover the brim,
   And nobody knew she was there.

   CHORUS

O'Reilly's Daughter

Traditional

♩ = 48 – first and last verses only

G

1. Sit-ting in O'Reil-ly's car one day, Tell-ing tales of

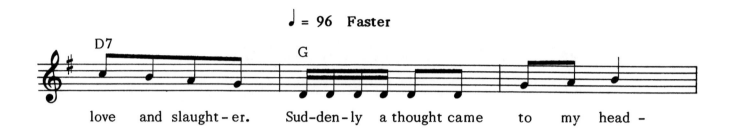

♩ = 96 Faster

D7   G

love and slaught-er. Sud-den-ly a thought came to my head –

D7   Chorus
                      G

Why not shag O'-Reil-ly's daughter. Yip-py-i – ay, yip-py-i – o,

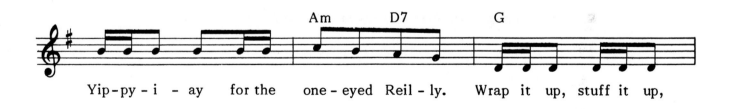

Am   D7   G

Yip-py-i – ay for the one-eyed Reil-ly. Wrap it up, stuff it up,

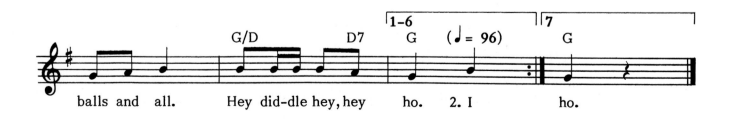

G/D   D7   1-6 G (♩ = 96)   7 G

balls and all. Hey did-dle hey, hey ho. 2. I   ho.

© 1991 International Music Publications

2. I dragged the maiden by the hand,
   Gently slipped my left leg over
   And never a word the maiden said –
   Laughed like hell 'til the fun was over!

   CHORUS

3. I heard a footstep on the stairs.
   Who should it be but the one-eyed Reilly,
   With two pistols in his hand,
   Looking for the man who shagged his daughter.

   CHORUS

4. Reilly took two shots at me –
   He missed me by an inch and a quarter.
   Hit the maiden, don't you know,
   Right in the place where she passes water.

   CHORUS

5. I grabbed O'Reilly by the curls,
   Stuffed his head in a bucket of water.
   Rammed two pistols up his arse
   A damn sight quicker, then I fucked his daughter.

   CHORUS

6. And now O'Reilly's dead and gone.
   Did they bury him? Not likely!
   They hung him to the shit house door.
   Now they bugger him twice nightly.

   CHORUS

7. And now O'Reilly's old and grey.
   And my prick is getting shorter.
   Still I dream of days of yore,
   When I fucked O'Reilly's daughter.

   CHORUS

Pickeldy, Pickeldy Pox

Traditional

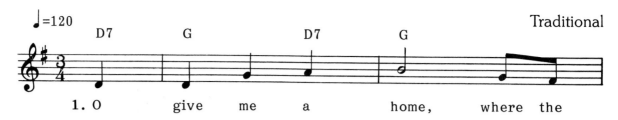

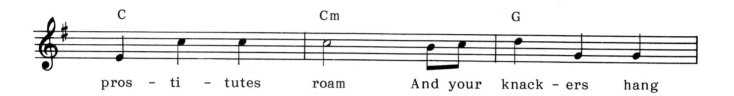

1. O give me a home, where the

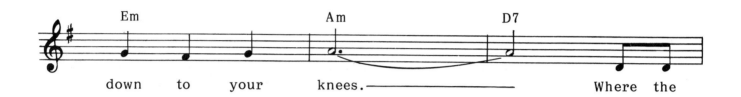

pros - ti - tutes roam And your knack - ers hang

down to your knees. Where the

ba - bies are born With a fif - teen inch

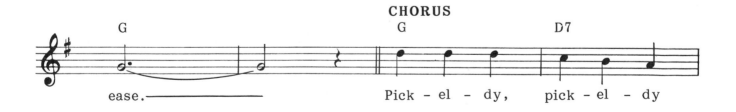

horn And the pox is the fav - 'rite dis -

CHORUS

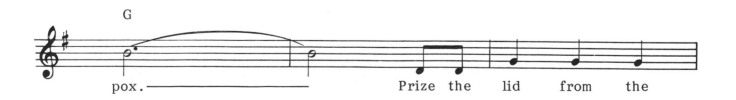

ease. Pick - el - dy, pick - el - dy

pox. Prize the lid from the

her —— ring box.———————— We are nev - er for -

lorn When we're hump - ing the whore At the

broth - el in East Grims - by docks.————

2. O give me a den that is mainly for men,

Where the whore house is full and foul.

When they take down their draws,

For the black sambo whores,

It's a darkness that knocks on your life.

CHORUS

3. The beds, they all creak

And the piss pots all leak,

And the sheets are not always too clean.

There's a hole in the wall,

For the lame and the poor

And the women are fucking machines.

CHORUS

Poor, But Honest

Traditional

♩ = 72

1. It was on a bridge at mid-night, Pick-ing blackheads from her

crotch. She said, "Sir, I've nev - er had it." I said,

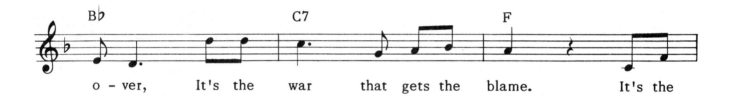

"Love, not fucking much!" It's the same the whole world

o - ver, It's the war that gets the blame. It's the

rich who get the plea-sure; Ain't it all a fucking shame.

2. It was on a bridge at midnight,
Throwing snowballs at the moon.
She said, "Sir, I've never had it;"
But she'd spoke too fucking soon.

CHORUS

3. She stood on the bridge at midnight;
She was looking rather good.
She had a puppy with her,
Licking up her menstrual blood.

CHORUS

© 1991 International Music Publications

The Red Flag

Traditional

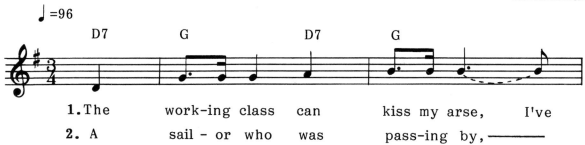

1. The work-ing class can kiss my arse, I've
2. A sail - or who was pass-ing by, —

got per - for - mance cajole at last. I'm out of work and
Tipped his hat and winked an eye. And then he saw to

on the dole, So stuff the flag right up your hole. 'Twas
his des-pair, She had a red flag fly-ing there.

on Gib-ral - ter's rocks so bare, I saw a maid - en ly-ing there. And

as she lay in sweet re-pose, a puff of wind blew up her clothes.

Quite Content With Masturbation

♩=126 **CHORUS**

Traditional

*_____ , nev-er heard of for-ni-ca-tion,

*_____ , nev-er dipped their tools. *_____ ,

quite con-tent with mas-tur-ba-tion - Thought a cunt was some-thing peo-ple

called them at school.— **Fine** 1. Now gath-er round and lis-ten boys a -

bout their big chief— He slaps his mas-sive pen-is in his

play-ers' teeth. His play-ers, they said may be at a

D.C. al Fine (last time)

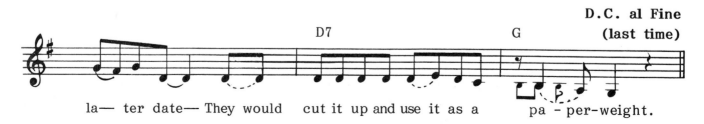

la— ter date— They would cut it up and use it as a pa-per-weight.

2. Now, *(insert name)* he is one massive man;
   It's a shame his little penis doesn't have the same span.
   When he taps off at a party and is all set to ride,
   He has to tie a plank to his backside.
   CHORUS

3. Now, *(insert name)* he is a *hooker*[**] quite fancy free;
   His lodger brings her cunt up with the morning tea.
   So many blokes had been in and out of there,
   A judge declared her cunt a public thoroughfare.
   CHORUS

4. Now, *(insert name)* he is the oldest player of the lot;
   He likes his women fresh straight from the cot.
   They're best when they are tight and a little bit tough –
   If they're old enough to bleed, they are bleeding old enough.
   CHORUS

NOTE: This song is about a rival team and is to be adapted accordingly:

* insert the name of the rival team.
** insert appropriate player position.

Rajah Of Astrakhan

Traditional

1. There was a Ra - jah of Ast - ra - khan, ya ho, ya ho. A most li - cen - ti - ous

fuck of a man, ya ho, ya ho. The

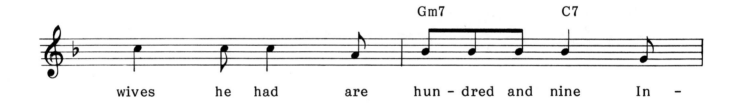

wives he had are hun - dred and nine In -

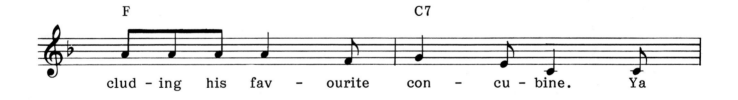

clud - ing his fav - ourite con - cu - bine. Ya

ho, you bug - gers, Ya ho, you bug - gers, Ya

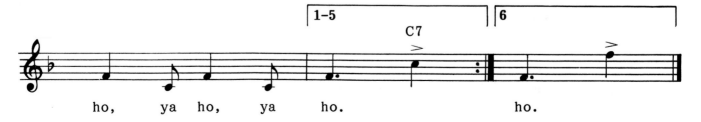

ho, ya ho, ya ho. ho.

2. One day he had a hell of a stand, ya ho, ya ho.
   He caught a warrior, one of his band, ya ho, ya ho.
   Go down to the harem you lazy swine
   And fetch my favourite concubine.
   Ya ho, you buggers...

3. The warrior fetched his concubine, ya ho, ya ho;
   A figure like Venus, a face divine, ya ho, ya ho.
   The Raj', he gave a significant grunt
   And passed his prick inside her cunt.
   Ya ho, you buggers...

4. The Rajah's cries were short and strong, ya ho, ya ho;
   The maiden's cries were loud and long, ya ho, ya ho.
   And just as the Rajah came to a head,
   They fell right through the fucking bed.
   Ya ho, you buggers...

5. They hit the ground with one hell of a thump, ya ho, ya ho;
   He completely buggered the poor girls cunt, ya ho, ya ho.
   And as for the Rajah's magnificent cock -
   It never recovered from the shock.
   Ya ho, you buggers...

6. There is a moral to this tale, ya ho, ya ho.
   There is a moral to this tale, ya ho, ya ho.
   If you will have a girl at all,
   Then have her up against the wall.
   Ya ho, you buggers...

Ring The Bell, Verger

Traditional

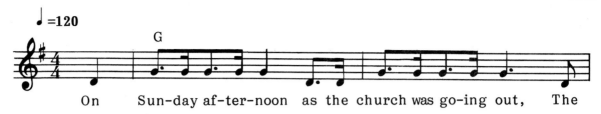

On Sun-day af-ter-noon as the church was go-ing out, The vic - ar said for fun; "I bet I've had more

women than you." And the cur - ate said, "You're on!" We'll

stand by the gate as the wo-men walk by And this shall be our

sign; You 'bing bong' for the women you've had And

The Sexual Life Of A Camel

Traditional

1. The— sex-u-al life of a ca-mel — Is

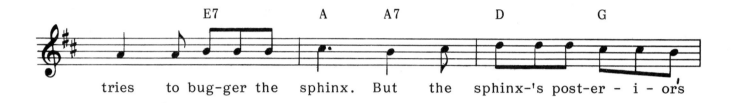

stranger than an-y-one thinks;—At the height of the mat-ing sea-son,— He

tries to bug-ger the sphinx. But the sphinx-'s post-er-i-or's

hard-er, — He's stuck on the sands on the Nile. — Which ac-

counts for the hump on the ca-mel,—And the sphinx-'s in-scru-ta-ble smile.

2. In the process of civilisation,
   From the anthropoid ape down to man;
   It is generally held that the navy,
   Has buggered whatever it can.
   Yet recent extensive researches
   By Darwin, and Hutsby and Hall,
   Conclusively prove that the hedgehog
   Has never been buggered at all.

3. We therefore believe our conclusion,
    Is incontrovertibly shown
    That the parietal safety of chipboard
    Is adjoined by the hedgehog alone.
    Why haven't they done it at Spithead?
    Have they done it at Harvard and Yale?
    And also at Oxford and Cambridge
    By shaving the spikes off its tail.

4. Singing bum ti ti, bum ti ti, titi bum,
    Titi bum ti ti, bum ti ti ay.
    Bum ti ti, bum ti ti, titi bum,
    Titi bum ti ti, bum ti ti ay.
    Oh, we're all queers together,
    Excuse us while we go upstairs.
    Yes, we're all queers together,
    That's why we go round in pairs.

5. My name is Cecil,
    I live in Leicester Square.
    I wear pink pyjamas
    And a rosebud in my hair.
    Oh, we're all queers together,
    Excuse us while we go upstairs.
    Yes, we're all queers together,
    That's why we go round in pairs.

6. I went for a ride in a "chuff chuff",
    It was crowded so I had to stand.
    A little boy offered me his seat,
    So I felt for it with my hand.
    Oh, we're all queers together,
    Excuse me while we go upstairs.
    Yes, we're all queers together,
    That's why we go round in pairs.

Sing Us Another One, Do

♩. = 60

Traditional

Chorus

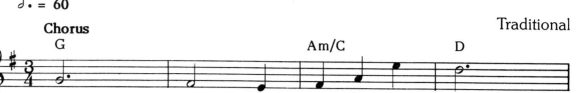

That was a hor - ri - ble song.

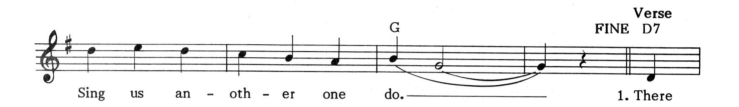

Sing us an - oth - er one, just like the oth - er one,

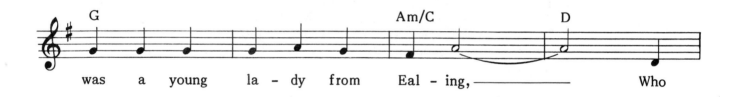

Sing us an - oth - er one do. — 1. There

was a young la - dy from Eal - ing, — Who

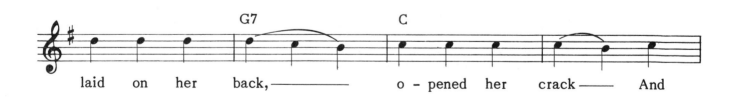

had a pe - cu - li - ar feel - ing, — So she

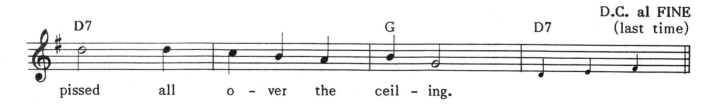

laid on her back, — o - pened her crack — And

pissed all o - ver the ceil - ing.

2. There was a young girl from Mobeal,
Whose cunt was made of blue steel;
She got all her thrills from pneumatic drills
And off-centred emery wheels.

CHORUS

3. There was a young vampire called Mabel,
With periods extremely stable;
One night at full moon she went down with a spoon
And drank herself under the table.

CHORUS

4. There was a young man called James,
Who delighted in peculiar games;
He lighted the rim of his grandmother's quim
And he laughed as she pissed through the flames.

CHORUS

5. There was a young girl called Hilda,
Who one night, went out with a builder;
He said that he could and he should, and he would -
When he didn't, he fucking near killed her.

CHORUS

6. There once was a lady called Annie,
Who had fleas, lice and crabs up her fanny;
To get up her flue was like touring the zoo;
There were wild beasts in each nook and cranny.

CHORUS

7. There was a young woman from France,
Who got on a bus in a trance;
Everyone fucked her except the conductor
And he came twice in his pants.

CHORUS

8. There was a young man from St. Paul's,
Who toured the music halls;
His favourite trick was to stand on his prick
And roll off the stage on his balls.

CHORUS

9. There was a musician from Rio,
Who seduced a dancer called Cleo,
As he slid off her panties she said, "No andantes;
I like it vivace con brio!"

CHORUS

10. A "do-it-yourselfer" called Alice,
Used a dynamite stick as a fallace;
They found her vagina in North Carolina,
Her tits up a tree in Dallas.

CHORUS

Sir Jasper

Traditional

1. Oh, Sir Jas-per do not touch me. Oh, Sir Jas-per do not

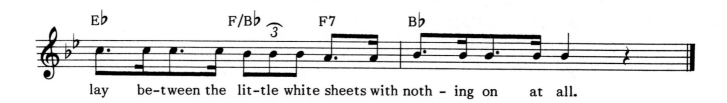

touch me. Oh, Sir Jas-per do not touch me. As she

lay be-tween the lit-tle white sheets with noth - ing on at all.

2. Oh, Sir Jasper do not touch.

   Oh, Sir Jasper do not touch.

   Oh, Sir Jasper do not touch.

   As she lay . . . .

3. Oh, Sir Jasper do not.

   Oh, Sir Jasper do not.

   Oh, Sir Jasper do not.

   As she lay . . . .

4. Oh, Sir Jasper do.

   Oh, Sir Jasper do.

   Oh, Sir Jasper do.

   As she lay . . . .

5. Oh, Sir Jasper.

   Oh, Sir Jasper.

   Oh, Sir Jasper.

   As she lay . . . .

6. Oh, Sir.

   Oh, Sir.

   Oh, Sir.

   As she lay . . . .

7. Oh.

   Oh.

   Oh.

   As she lay . . . .

8. She's a most immoral lady.

   She's a most immoral lady.

   She's a most immoral lady.

   As she lay . . . .

Note: When singing verses two to seven, omit the last word of lines one to three of the preceeding verse, as directed. The omitted beats should be counted in silence.

The Road To Gundigi

♩ =104

Traditional

There's a track winding back from her arse-hole to her crack, along the

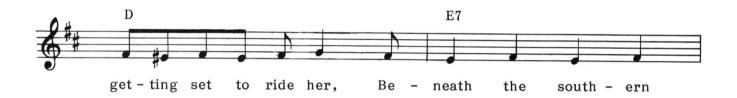

road to Gund-ig - i.   There's an   Aus-si down beside her, who's

get - ting set to ride her,   Be - neath the south - ern

skies.   With a   "frenchy" on his doo - dle,   he

rides her with ease,   As he   mo-tions up her crack-ie with the

ac-tion of his knees.   And the   time will come to pass,   When he

whops it up her arse, A-long the   road to Gund-ig - i.

The Tampax Factory

Traditional

1. You can tell by the smell That she is-n't ve-ry well, When the

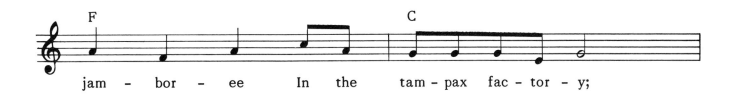

end of the month comes a - round. **Chorus:** Let's have a

jam - bor - ee In the tam - pax fac - tor - y;

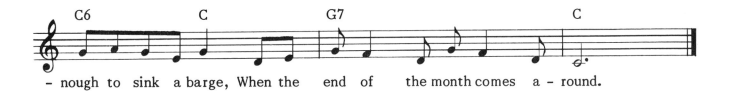

Shout out your ord-ers loud and clear. Make them small, make them large, Make e -

- nough to sink a barge, When the end of the month comes a - round.

2. You can tell by the moaning
   That she's losing haemoglobin,
   When the end of the month comes around.

   CHORUS

3. You can tell by the stench
   That she's got a septic trench,
   When the end of the month comes around.

   CHORUS

4. You can tell when she slips
   That there's blood loss through her lips,
   When the end of the month comes around.

   CHORUS

There Was An Old Lady

Traditional

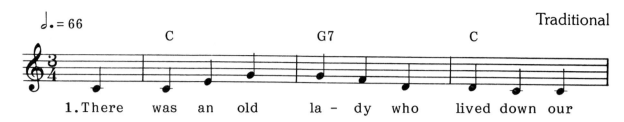

1. There was an old la - dy who lived down our street, She got con - sti - pa - tion from

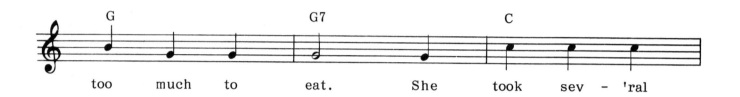

too much to eat. She took sev - 'ral

pills on a Sat - ur - day night And—

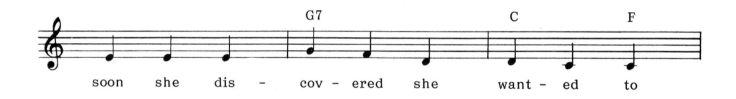

soon she dis - cov - ered she want - ed to

CHORUS

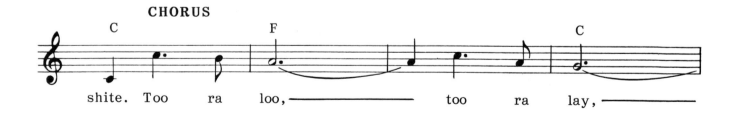

shite. Too ra loo, —— too ra lay, ——

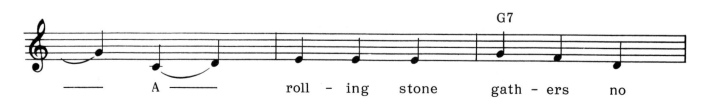

—— A —— roll - ing stone gath - ers no

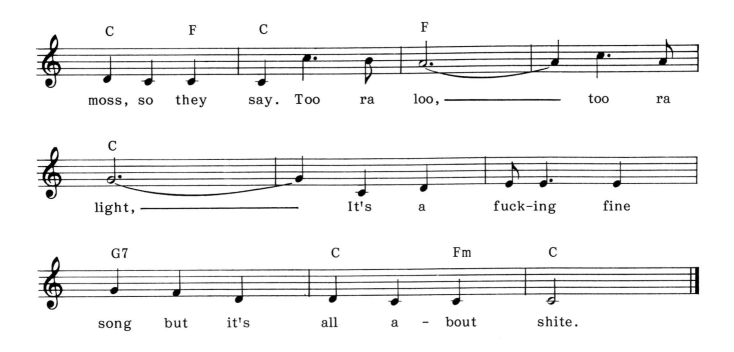

moss, so they say. Too ra loo, ———— too ra

light, ———————— It's a fuck-ing fine

song but it's all a - bout shite.

2. She went to a window and stuck out her arse,
   And just then her landlord should happen to pass.
   He heard a loud noise as he looked up on high,
   And a fucking great turd hit him right in the eye.
   CHORUS

3. He looked to the North and he looked to the South,
   And a fucking great log landed right in his mouth.
   He looked to the East and he looked to the West,
   And another great log landed right on his chest.
   CHORUS

4. The next time you walk over Battersea Bridge,
   Look out for a watchman asleep on the edge.
   He's dressed with a placard; upon it is writ:
   "Be kind to the Welshman who's minding my shit."
   CHORUS

Von Spearo

Traditional

Oh, my name is Von Spearo and I come from a-far.

Hey, Von Spear - o, * Von Spear - o. I o-pen my mu-sic box and

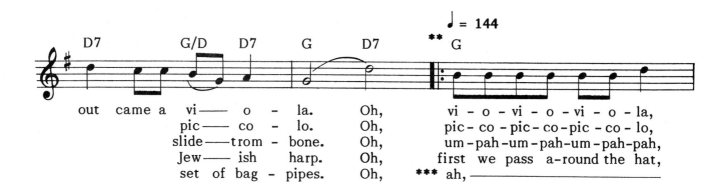

out came a vi —— o - la. Oh, vi - o - vi - o - vi - o - la,
pic —— co - lo. Oh, pic - co - pic - co - pic - co - lo,
slide ——trom - bone. Oh, um - pah-um - pah-um - pah-pah,
Jew —— ish harp. Oh, first we pass a-round the hat,
set of bag - pipes. Oh, *** ah, ——————————

(F when bagpipes)   (F when bagpipes)

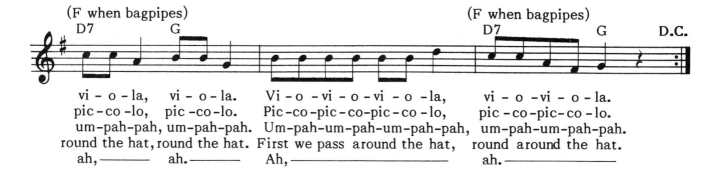

vi - o - la, vi - o - la. Vi - o -vi - o-vi - o - la, vi - o -vi - o - la.
pic-co-lo, pic -co-lo. Pic-co-pic-co-pic-co -lo, pic -co-pic-co - lo.
um-pah-pah, um-pah-pah. Um-pah-um-pah-um-pah-pah, um-pah-um-pah-pah.
round the hat, round the hat. First we pass around the hat, round around the hat.
ah, ——— ah.——— Ah, —————————— ah. ———

* Blow a raspberry

** Repeat these bars, in reverse order, as necessary

*** Sing 'ah' while pinching the nose for effect. Tap your throat
with the side of the other hand to the rhythm.

Whatawank

Traditional

Whose Are They?

Traditional

As I tried on a full dress suit to go to a full dress ball. The jack - et, it was far too short; the trou - sers, far too tall. And so to make the bas-tard's fit, I cut off a yard or so. And as I waltzed a - round the floor, I heard the peo - ple say; And as I waltzed a - round the floor, I heard the peo - ple say: "You're loos - ing them, you're loos - ing them! Lift up your trou-sers high. Whose are they? Whose are they? My God, they're-one hell of a sight. Whose are they? Whose are——they? My God, they're-one hell of a sight.

Why Was He Born?

The Woodpecker's Song

Traditional

2. I removed my finger from the woodpecker's hole
And the woodpecker said, "God bless my soul!
Put it back, put it back, put it back,
Replace it."

3. I replaced my finger in the woodpecker's hole
And the woodpecker said, "God bless my soul!
Turn it round, turn it round, turn it round,
Revolve it."

4. I revolved my finger in the woodpecker's hole
And the woodpecker said, "God bless my soul!
In and out, in and out, in and out,
Reciprocate it."

5. I reciprocated my finger in the woodpecker's hole
And the woodpecker said, "God bless my soul!
Pull it out, pull it out, pull it out,
Retract it."

6. I retracted my finger from the woodpecker's hole
And the woodpecker said, "God bless my soul!
Take a whiff, take a whiff, take a whiff;
Revolting!"

MEMORIES

OF A

RUGBY CLUB

Shirley Wanderers
R.F.C.

Printed in England
Panda Press · Haverhill · Suffolk • 10/91